GOHN DAGOW

Movements for Health and Self Defense

by F.H. Treon and D.G. Hickmond

Published by
Flowing Dragon Productions

It is not intended that the reader master the techniques in this book without the aid of a certified Gohn Dagow teacher or instructor.

The writers of Gohn Dagow Movements for Health and Self Defense accept no legal responsibility for injury, accidental or intentional, resulting from practicing or using any of the techniques in this book.

Library of Congress Cataloging in Publication Data

Library of Congress Catalog Number: 86-82317

Publisher's ISBN: 0-9617439-0-5

Treon, F.H. and Hickmond, D.G.
Gohn dagow movements for health and self defense
Includes indexes
First Edition

Printed by: Maverick Publications
Drawer 5007
Bend, OR 97708

Published by: Flowing Dragon Productions
P.O. Box 3238
Ashland, OR 97520 USA

ACKNOWLEDGEMENTS

We would like to thank the following people, without whom this book would not be possible.

My mother Marion C. Treon for my early spiritual training. My daughter Christina Bowers for her love and support. My teachers. My students over the years, who are also my teachers. Special thanks to instructors Richard May, Charles Draper, and Michael Lucero.

J. H. Treon III

Futzu Liu Suzy

My parents Orville and Christine Hickmond for their love, wisdom, and patience. My wife Laura and children Nathaniel and Gwen for their love, understanding, patience, and support. My students and teachers.

Special thanks to Daniel Beougher for his dedication and expert typesetting. Special thanks to Steve Finck for his many contributions, especially paper.

D. B. Hickmond
Sien Seong Haw

Art and Photo Credits:

Thanks to Lilian Chu for her Chinese calligraphy.

Thanks to Rosanna Hart for her picture *Parting the Clouds* on page 43.

F.H. Treon III
Futzu Liu Suzy

Daniel G. Hickmond
Sien Seong Haw

About the Authors

Futzu Francis Treon was born Francis Harry Treon III in Scranton, Pennsylvania in 1929. At age eight his pelvis was crushed by a truck. While on crutches, he was the target of local bullies who took away his crutches and beat him with them. This mistreatment motivated him to leave home at age fifteen to study with a teacher whose philosophies of truth, justice, and honor were similar to his own. He discovered Grandmaster Chin Li in Phoenix, Arizona in 1945 and began to study Gohn Dagow. After years of training he became a Sien Seong (teacher), and in 1965 he became a Futzu (Master).

From 1949 to 1970 Futzu Treon taught the martial aspects of Gohn Dagow to the military as a member of the military and as a civilian. He trained representatives of the Security Department at Sandia Labs in Albuquerque, New Mexico and other government agencies. He founded the American Gohn Dagow Association.

After 1970 Futzu Treon assumed full-time responsibilities as the Master of Gohn Dagow. He established the International Center for Gohn Dagow. The Center was featured on National Educational Television in December 1971. He is the present director of the American Gohn Dagow Association.

In 1985 Futzu Treon moved to the beautiful Colestin Valley near Ashland, Oregon. His center is on nine acres with a pond and two year-round streams in the midst of century-old pine and fir trees.

Daniel Hickmond was born in Fresno, California in 1946. He received an M.A. in English Literature from California State University Fresno in 1975. Mr. Hickmond became Sien Seong in 1986 after studying with Futzu Treon for thirteen years. Sien Seong Hickmond currently teaches Gohn Dagow in Bend, Oregon.

CONTENTS

Introduction

This book was written to help preserve some of the fundamental movements and philosophies of Gohn Dagow, an ancient and beautiful, yet dying art. Oral tradition has it that Gohn Dagow was derived from martial art forms that date back to 2800 B.C. Gohn Dagow is an ancient, classical, southern Chinese, soft, monk form. However, to place Gohn Dagow within the martial art tradition through written, historical evidence is impossible. Nevertheless, some comparisons of Gohn Dagow to other martial arts may help edify the student's understanding of Gohn Dagow. A comprehensive, historical study of Gohn Dagow, as part of the martial arts tradition, is not intended here. Our aim is to deal with Gohn Dagow and what it is.

CHAPTER I

The 1000 Mile Journey

In the Chinese martial arts various schools and fighting techniques developed partly because of different styles and philosophies. The terms *soft* and *hard* refer to different styles; the terms *monk* and *warrior* refer to different philosophies. Gohn Dagow is a soft, monk form, but to understand Gohn Dagow, it is essential to understand the meaning of *soft* and *hard*, and *monk* and *warrior*.

Soft style movements are different from *hard* style movements. *Soft* styles emphasize internal power; *hard* styles emphasize external, physical power.

Hard styles mainly display tense, sharp, rigid movements. Soft styles exemplify flowing motions. Tremendous speed can be developed in both styles, but tension helps create rigidity. Soft styles emphasize internal power, *chi*. They may also teach the development of extraordinary physical strength and body conditioning, *kung*. Although hard styles emphasize external, physical power, they may also teach self-control and the development of chi.

The soft and hard styles may have had similar origins. However, the lack of empirical evidence proving their origins discourages the notion that all forms were derived from any one original form or from any one teacher. Moreover, another distinction regarding martial arts in general is the philosophical difference between the way of the warrior and the way of the monk. Just as the origins of hard and soft styles may be similar, origins of monk and warrior forms may also be similar. Again, there is no way to verify such an assertion. It is important to recognize that for centuries the two forms have been separate. While soft and hard styles exist in both monk and warrior forms, most monk philosophies recognize: humility as a virtue; the relativity of good and evil, right and wrong; that the universe and the human condition are in a constant state of change; that all life is precious; and that the individual possesses a high degree of integrity.

Many Gohn Dagow philosophies are based on religions such as Buddhism, Taoism, and Confucianism. Some precepts of the *Old* and *New Testament* are incorporated into Gohn Dagow. Numerous philosophies were also originated and passed on by various masters. In the monk forms, the highest emphasis is placed on spiritual and mental development and on raising one's consciousness. Physical self-defense is used only as a last resort to self-preservation. *If you truly respect life, you will learn to preserve it.*

The way of the monk was less agressive than the way of the warrior. The monk forms taught high regard for human life. If someone blocked the monk's path, he would walk around them. If someone blocked the warrior's path, he was obligated to knock them off the path. Those people practicing monk forms used their knowledge only for self-defense.

The soft styles stress mental, physical, and spiritual *flowing*, which are all integrally related. Mental control and the ability to float the mind have applications that extend far beyond instances requiring self-defense. They are useful in preventing situations that might require self-defense. They are valuable in dealing with daily personal and emotional problems. If one is truly in touch with his higher consciousness, he will flow in life as he should.

Mental or intellectual *flowing* means knowing what to do; that is, accurately perceiving and assessing all aspects of a martial or non-martial situation. The *Yin-Yang* philosophy, *nothing is so permanent as never to change*, exemplifies the principle of flowing. Flowing means changing and learning to change. Studying Gohn Dagow is a means of fully developing awareness: that is, learning to flow.

Physical *flowing* includes several things: acting in harmony with mental *flowing*; executing the proper movement at the proper time; and moving smoothly from one technique to another, maintaining complete harmony between the student and his environment.

Instinct can play an effective role in developing the ability to flow physically. There is, however, a conscious effort to avoid blindly conditioning reflexes. The blocks and blows should flow together so smoothly that only a trained eye would discern when one stops and the other begins. Gohn Dagow philosophies stress all aspects of self-control.

Spiritual *flowing* is communicating with and acting in harmony with the essence of one's being to stay in balance with the universe. Spiritual flowing has meant many things. Such terminology may imply that Gohn Dagow is a religion; but it is not. Nevertheless, spiritual involvement is available for those who desire it. Whether or not the student involves himself in spiritual matters, the sense of flowing with the universe coincides with the sense of physical and mental flowing already discussed.

Learning to flow physically, mentally, and spiritually teaches self-discipline and control, and it improves health. Gohn Dagow is a way for each person to develop strength, power, balance, coordination, agility, and flexibility. Gohn Dagow offers methods for: strengthening, toning, and thickening muscles and tendons; preventing bone and muscle deterioration; relaxing muscles. There are movements to relax the back, shoulders, and hips and to relieve stiffness and discomfort associated with arthritis and bursitis. There are techniques to build endurance, strengthen the cardiovascular system, cleanse the respiratory system, balance the breath and circulation, and release energy blocks. Physical, mental, and spiritual flowing combine with health and self defense to develop a totally balanced individual.

The yin-yang exemplifies the balance and harmony of the universe reflected in the physical, mental, and spiritual balance within each person. Self-control is one result of that balance. The meditations and philosophies of Gohn Dagow, combined with the physical techniques and dances (called *kilmos*), develop a complete, balanced individual. Gohn Dagow is an ancient, classical Chinese form of self-defense that develops the mind, body, and spirit. Those persons interested in total self-development and in raising their consciousness make the best Gohn Dagow students.

流 水

Flowing Water

I will yield and flow around resistance as the water in a stream flows around a rock.

In Gohn Dagow mental control is achieved by: learning and practicing the physical techniques and dances; meditating; and learning and applying the philosophies. A beginning student receives only basic meditations, some of which will be discussed later. The meditations help the student contact his inner energy, the *chi.* Mental acuity increases because it is necessary to concentrate when learning new dances and techniques. To a new student the Gohn Dagow movements are new and thus potentially difficult. The student must perform the movements in a precise manner. After learning new techniques, the student should be able to stop concentrating, float his mind, and flow. Regardless of how long one studies, concentration remains an integral part of the art, although movements become easier to learn the longer one studies.

Another distinction worth noting, although it does not relate to the stylistic differences between soft and hard, is that Gohn Dagow is primarily a *short arm* rather than a *long arm* form. Short arm forms could be either hard or soft, monk or warrior. Short arm means close-in fighting. Long arm means long-range fighting. For example, a short arm technique would include a forward step with the left foot and a blow with the right hand. A long arm technique would mean a step with the right foot and a blow with the right hand.

Gohn Dagow, and other systems, incorporates both short arm and long arm techniques. Gohn Dagow is primarily a short arm, southern Chinese system using hand, elbow, knee, and head techniques. People in the South were usually shorter and more agrarian than those in the North. Thus, they adapted a close-range style conducive to their stature and to the flatter and sometimes marshy terrain. In northern China, where the terrain was generally more mountainous and the people taller, the long arm forms with high kicks and long punches were more practical.

峡　谷

Empty Canyon

A wise man speaks not into an empty canyon to hear the echo of his own voice; rather, he speaks into the canyon of your mind, and plants the seeds of thought so that they may grow and become action.

Since written historical evidence is scanty at best for the martial arts in general and non-existent regarding Gohn Dagow in particular, we must rely on oral tradition for the information we have. Oral tradition has it that Gohn Dagow centered within the secrecy of religious temples until about 638 A.D., when a monk named Chin Li brought the art out of the obscurity of the temple. The art was most popular between the seventh and thirteenth centuries, during the relatively peaceful and culturally active Tang-Sung era. Before that time the hostile nature of the times and people prohibited popularizing Gohn Dagow. Other hard forms and warrior forms were easier to learn. The warrior philosophy was also more in harmony with the aggressive intentions of many war lords.

Both monk and warrior forms are laden with tradition, and Gohn Dagow is no different. Its philosophies, customs, and even the name abound with tradition. Formally, the name of the art represents: the man credited with bringing the art out of the temple; the era during which it received most acclaim; and the kind of art. Gohn Dagow means soft fighting, soft way, or gentle way. The formal name of the art is thus:

Chin Li - Tang Sung - Gohn Dagow.

Because modern Gohn Dagow practitioners still maintain many ancient customs and traditions of the art as a monk form, they do not commercialize the art. The only living master still emphasizes developing patience and balancing physical, mental, and spiritual training and discipline. Instructor fees are minimal. It is not a sport form, and there are no belts, tournaments, or trophies. Since it is not a sport form, students wear black uniforms instead of white. The student is always aware that he is judged by what he is and how he performs, not by what he wears.

However, sashes are worn. There are only three colors: black, orange, and red. The processes of acquiring the sash differ from the methods of earning belts in most sport forms. It may be years before a student receives a material symbol of his progress or skill. The way the sash is worn, as well as its color, reflects the student's standing within the art. The master ties his sash in the center of the waist. The male student ties his on the left side of the waist. The female student ties hers on the right side of the waist. Although one is a lifetime student of the art, in the classroom the student wears the black sash for approximately fifteen years. After that time, and after passing tests established by the master, a student may become a teacher and wear the orange sash. After twenty years, and after passing established tests, a student may become a master and wear the red sash.

The yin-yang, with the green dragon above it, is the traditional emblem of Gohn Dagow. It represents balance, harmony, and unity. Modern Gohn Dagow students strive for physical, mental, and spiritual harmony in the art and in life. Hopefully, Gohn Dagow students will flow smoothly and gracefully in all things, just as the majestic green dragon floats above the clouds, ensuring the prevalence of truth, justice, and honor.

落葉

Falling Leaf

As the leaf falls from the tree,
it nurtures the tree from which it came,
or it may be carried on the wind
to nurture the ground elsewhere.

Sapling Bent

As the sapling is bent,
so grows the tree.

CHAPTER II
The Dancer and the Dance

Although Gohn Dagow is a monk form and may have been characterized by one religious system, which is now unknown, the art is not now dominated by any one religious philosophy. Over the years certain philosophies and ethical concepts of Buddhism, Taoism, Confucianism, and Christianity have been absorbed into the system. It remains, however, a monk form.

Gohn Dagow practitioners do not teach that Gohn Dagow is the only method of self-defense or self-actualization. Instead, Gohn Dagow teachers maintain that each person is an individual seeking his own path up the mountain of life. Each self-defense form has its own advantages. One form is not inherently better or worse than another. The philosophy of *The Mountain* embodies that principle as its theme.

山面

面南

北

Mountain - North Side/South Side

A wise man sat on a mountain top observing two climbers, one approaching from the north, one from the south side of the mountain. The climber on the north side was dressed for the cold weather, and the climber on the south side was dressed for warm. As the climbers reached a point where each could see the other, they began arguing endlessly about who was properly dressed for the climb. The one said it was cold and warned the other to prepare accordingly. He in turn said it was hot on his side and the other was improperly dressed. They remained immobile, each on his own path, arguing forever. The wise man, observing the entire episode, knew that each climber was right in his own way.

Just as the wise man knew that each individual must find his own path up the mountain, let us begin our study of Gohn Dagow.

The Salutation is the first, most basic movement learned in Gohn Dagow. It has several meanings. It is a greeting when students meet each other or the teacher. Students perform the greeting at the beginning and at the end of classes and workouts. Classes and workouts open and close with *The Salutation.* It is a gesture of apology and a symbol of accepting an apology. Formal kilmos (dances) open and close with *The Salutation.* It is a gesture of hello and good-bye. *The Salutation* also means *I bow to no man, but I bow to the divinity within every man. The Salutation* means to come or to go in peace.

The Salutation is a graceful, simple movement. However, to an untrained eye, the beauty of the movement obscures its meaning as a self-defense technique. There are no wasted movements in Gohn Dagow. Its movements have been perfected in centuries past. It is the student's responsibility to strive for that perfection. Each movement has a definite purpose and a specific meaning and tradition. Even this first movement embodies the mental and physical balance of the yin-yang. *The Salutation* reveals the flowing motions that identify Gohn Dagow as soft fighting. When *The Salutation* is done without thought, it is a moving meditation.

The Salutation

1. Stand in a ready posture (Figure A). Relax the body and hands, palms of the hands facing the thighs. Keep the feet flat and parallel, comfortably spread so the insides of the feet are about hip width apart. The knees are slightly bent, shoulders relaxed yet erect, back straight yet not rigid, head up, eyes forward.

Figure A.

2. Rotate the hands so the palms face forward (Figure B). Keeping the hands straight in line with the forearms, raise the hands and forearms out and up from the sides of the body, keeping the elbows close to the body, yet not tight against it.

Figure B.

3. As the hands begin to meet, bring the left foot to the right (Figure C), so the two are touching (Figure D). If possible, the sides of the feet, knees, and thighs of the left leg should touch those of the right.

Figure C.

4. Bring the hands together in front of the body, thumbs touching the body, forearms parallel to the ground (Figure D).

Figure D.

The hands and feet should touch at the same time. Another meaning of the *Yin-Yang* philosophy is that *knowledge* (symbolized by the right direction) *does not seek ignorance* (symbolized by the left direction). Thus, bring the left foot to the right, symbolizing the individual's search for knowledge. There is a slight pause the instant the hands and feet touch. Cock the head slightly forward. Keep the eyes forward and alert (Figure D). This is not a bow. All people are equal in Gohn Dagow; one person does not bow to another.

The posture now formed (Figure D) represents the meanings mentioned previously. This position also resembles a gesture of prayer, and it implies a degree of vulnerability. However, another meaning of the *Yin-Yang* is that evil may exist in good and vice-versa. *Expect goodness in all men, but be prepared for evil.* Thus, the eyes are open, and the individual is alert, ready for any possible threat.

Figure E.

5. Continue the circular motion separating the hands downward, returning the hands to the sides. Simultaneously replace the left foot in its starting place and lift the head (Figure E).

6. Hands stop at the sides, palms parallel to the ground, fingers pointing forward (Figure F). The movement is now complete.

Figure F.

The student should execute this movement flowing continuously, smoothly, and slowly. When the feet touch and the head is cocked, there is a slight pause while waiting for the gesture to be returned. Except for this brief pause, the movement is continuous and circular. Practice Steps A through F in a continuous succession, stopping only for a pause (Figure D).

It is important that the forearms and hands circle to exemplify the flowing motion and to block possible hand or foot attacks. Now *The Salutation* is clearly seen as more than merely a peaceful gesture. It is a two-fold defense technique. The eyes are alert, and the circling hands and forearms are blocks.

In performing *The Salutation,* inhale as the hands go from Figure A to a point just past Figure B, where the forearms are parallel to the ground. Exhale from this point until the hands and feet touch (Figure D).

Specific breathing methods for each individual technique will not be discussed in this text. However, general breathing patterns are described below. So, the student may wish to ensure he understands the material here before learning each movement that follows; or he may desire to consult the explanation of breathing control below as he learns subsequent techniques. In any case, proper breathing is important to receive maximum benefits from all the movements.

Generally, exhale when *advancing*, inhale when *yielding* (*advancing* and *yielding* are discussed on page 61). Exhale with kicks and strikes, inhale with blocks. Exhale with the forward momentum of a step, kick, or strike. When more than one strike or kick is used in a technique, inhale with the initial block and a single exhale is used for all forward-moving techniques that follow.

In addition to the meanings of *The Salutation* already mentioned, *The Salutation* represents still another ancient philosophy: *The Polished Mirror*. The hands at the sides, palms down (Figure F, page 22), symbolizes a mirror that reflects the individual's total being.

擦亮

鏡子

Polished Mirror

*My mind is as a mirror polished a thousand times.
I will strive to honor the art, my teacher, and not
to harm my fellow man.*

When an individual polishes his mirror, it means he is at peace with himself and the universe. Polishing one's mirror symbolizes personal control over one's thoughts, emotions, and actions.

Thus, *The Salutation* is also *Polishing the Mirror*. Even if one is alone, giving *The Salutation* at the beginning and end of a workout acknowledges the art and its traditions. Performing *The Salutation* also helps enter the proper mental state so one can do the dances and techniques correctly. It is also a healing movement that balances and centers the body's energies by clearing and focusing the mind. Workouts should not be pious activities, but they should be done seriously, striving to perfect physical techniques and develop consciousness.

After *The Salutation*, the next movement learned in Gohn Dagow is *Parting the Clouds*. This kilmo (dance) exemplifies the symbolically undefeatable green dragon, alert and poised with its head and shoulders above the clouds, flowing through the clouds, brushing them aside without disturbing them. When one performs this seemingly simple dance correctly, it symbolizes the main principles of the art: flowing motion; self control; and physical, mental, and spiritual balance.

Parting the Clouds is a physical activity for improving health and a self-defense technique. The mental and physical effort required to learn this movement build patience, discipline, and control. It is also a meditation, but before meditating on the movement, the student must master it physically.

For improving health, *Parting the Clouds* is a clearing exercise that removes the cobwebs of doubt and indecision. It balances the breath and circulation. It releases energy blocks and relieves physical and emotional stress and strain. It can relieve sinus congestion and minor headaches.

For self defense, *Parting the Clouds* is a blocking sequence. It also teaches the student the basic directional pattern all subsequent kilmos in Gohn Dagow follow. In Gohn Dagow, as in many ancient arts, the organizational pattern for dances follows the eight major compass directions: east, southeast, south, southwest, west, northwest, north, and northeast. The student executes the dance first to the right, then to the left, emphasizing the *Yin-Yang* philosophy that knowledge (yang, represented by the right direction) goes before ignorance (yin, represented by the left direction). However, before learning the formal kilmo, the student must learn the foot movements first, then the hand movements. After both are learned, they will be combined.

For meditation, *Parting the Clouds* is a means of contacting the inner energy, *the chi*. It is a method of discovering inner peace and peace with the universe. It is a way to learn flowing motion, self control, and physical, mental, and spiritual balance.

Parting the Clouds *(Foot Movements to the Right)*

Figure A.

1. Stand in a ready posture facing east, explained earlier in *The Salutation* (Figure A).

2. Pivot on the center of the right foot while stepping with the left foot in front of and perpendicular to the right, forming a "T" stance to the east. *This is a right hand posture*, so named because in ancient times one stood with the left foot forward, shield in the left hand, weapon in the right hand (if one was right handed) (Figure B).

Figure B.

Do not be afraid to step out into a comfortable stance, feet hip-width apart, knees slightly bent, centering the weight, balancing it equally between the feet. The trunk should remain upright, relaxed. There should be no tension in the body. The head should be erect, eyes looking straight ahead, yet not focused on anything particular. Facing east is significant because the sun rises in the East, symbolizing the light source, as well as the source of knowledge.

Figure C.

3. Pivot on the centers of both feet 180° to the west, re-forming the "T" stance with the right foot perpendicular to the left (Figure C).

4. Step with the left foot to the south, keeping the right foot stationary and re-forming the "T" stance, left foot perpendicular to the right (Figure D).

Figure D.

5. Pivot on the centers of both feet 180° to the north, re-forming the "T" with the right foot perpendicular to the left (Figure E).

Figure E.

6. Step with the left foot to the southwest, simultaneously pivoting slightly on the center of the right foot to re-form the "T" (Figure F).

Figure F.

7. Pivot on the centers of both feet 180° to the northeast, re-forming the "T" stance with the right foot perpendicular to the left (Figure G).

Figure G.

8. Step with the left foot to the northwest, re-forming the "T" stance (Figure H). There is no need to pivot on the right foot.

Figure H.

9. Pivot on the centers of both feet 180° to the southeast re-forming the "T" stance (Figure I).

10. Step with the left foot back to the east into the home position, pivoting slightly on the right foot so the toes of both feet point straight ahead, insides of the feet hip-width apart, the ready posture (Figure A).

Figure I.

When the student can move to the right smoothly, without jerks or stops, gently flowing from one position to the next, attempt the movement to the left.

Parting the Clouds *(Foot Movements to the Left)*

Figure J.

1. Stand in the ready posture facing east (Figure J).

Figure K.

2. Pivot on the center of the left foot while stepping with the right foot in front of and perpendicular to the left, forming a "T" stance to the east (Figure K). *This is a left hand posture.*

Figure L.

3. Pivot on the centers of both feet 180° to the west, re-forming the "T" stance (Figure L).

4. Step with the right foot to the north, keeping the left foot stationary and re-forming the "T" stance, right foot perpendicular to the left (Figure M).

Figure M.

5. Pivot on the centers of both feet 180° to the south, re-forming the "T" stance (Figure N).

Figure N.

6. Step with the right foot to the northwest, simultaneously pivoting slightly on the center of the left foot, re-forming the "T" stance (Figure O).

Figure O.

7. Pivot on the centers of both feet 180° to the southeast, re-forming the "T" stance, left foot perpendicular to the right (Figure P).

Figure P.

8. Step with the right foot to the southwest, re-forming the "T" stance (Figure Q). There is no need to pivot on the left foot.

Figure Q.

9. Pivot on the centers of both feet 180° to the northeast, re-forming the "T" stance (Figure R).

Figure R.

10. Step with the right foot back to the east into the home position, pivoting slightly on the left foot so the toes of both feet point straight ahead, insides of the feet hip-width apart, the ready posture (Figure S).

Figure S.

The balls of the feet should always contact the ground first, then the heel, stepping with the toes pointed. The student should not exaggerate the step; the foot should glide smoothly, only slightly above the ground. The student should be relaxed, but not limp, maintaining control. Practice until there are no stops, jerks, or hesitations, until the movements flow from one to another smoothly yet precisely. Then put the left and right directions together, doing them both as one flowing motion.

Adding the hand movements to the foot movements makes this kilmo complete and more difficult. So before combining the two, the hand movements must be learned separately.

Parting the Clouds *(Hand Movements)*

Maintain the hand height and distance from the head, shown below in Figures A and B, whenever *Parting the Clouds.* Notice that in both Figures A and B, the fingers are extended and joined, yet not rigid. The correct distance between the hands is maintained by the following check (refer to Figure B): The extended thumb of the right hand should touch the chin. The extended little finger of the right hand should touch the extended thumb of the left hand. The left hand is slightly higher than the right. Do not extend the hands way out in front of the face; keep them at a comfortable distance.

Figure A.

Figure B.

1. Stand in the ready posture (Figure C).

Figure C.

2. Rotate the hands so the palms face forward. Keeping the hands straight in line with the forearms, raise the hands and forearms out and up from the sides of the body. Keep the elbows close to the body, but not tight against it. Continue moving the hands until the left hand is in front of and in line with the right hand. The hands move in a circular manner to block the face. Both hands are in line with the nose. The right hand is between the left hand and the face. The fingertips of the left hand should be above eyebrow level, elbows bent comfortably. The fingertips of the right hand should be slightly below those of the left, about nose level (Figures D, E, and F). Maintain proper distance between hands and face by re-checking hand position as shown in Figures A and B page 36. Relax; do not tense the shoulders. Experiment until the hands feel naturally at ease in this position. *This is a right hand posture also.*

Figure D.

Figure E.

Right hand posture and left hand posture are common positions used often in Gohn Dagow. Henceforth, right hand posture and left hand posture will mean the combined hand and foot movements for each posture already learned; i.e. right hand posture is left foot forward, left hand forward; left hand posture is right foot forward, right hand forward. The right hand posture is shown in Figure F at right and on page 39, Figure B. The left hand posture is shown on page 38, Figure H, and on page 40, Figure E.

Figure F.

3. Keeping the right hand and forearm vertical, shift them slightly to the right. While keeping the left hand and forearm as vertical as possible, move them from the shoulder across the chest from left to right while bringing them closer to the chest. The left hand passes between the right hand and the face (Figure G). Then move the right hand and forearm in front of the left hand, right to left, slightly passing the left hand. Stop the right hand in the position originally occupied by the left hand (Figure H). *This is a left hand posture.*

Figure G.

4. The left hand (Figure H) is at the height of the right hand (Figure F), and the right hand (Figure H) is at the height of the left hand (Figure F). Now merely reverse the hand movements to return to the right hand posture, i.e. left hand in front of the right (Figure F).

Figure H.

If both hands do not move as described, the resulting position will be cramped and awkward. There will be little room for the left hand beside the right hand. The shoulders will be tense and movement will be limited. The hands and arms should flow smoothly in a soft motion, emulating moving clouds. Practice this blocking movement slowly from the ready posture, gradually increasing speed. There should be no tension in the body, particularly none in the hands, forearms, or shoulders.

Parting the Clouds *(Right Hand Posture)*

After learning the hand techniques, the student is ready to combine them with the foot movements. As earlier, the student performs the movement to the right first, following the same stepping pattern as before. Now the movement is a formal kilmo or dance. Observe the following breathing pattern for *Parting the Clouds*: inhale while the first *Circle Block* moves to the nose. As it passes the nose, begin exhaling. Continue exhaling until the second hand completes its movement.

Figure A.

1. Stand in the ready posture facing east (Figure A).

Figure B.

2. Rotate the hands so the palms face forward. Raise the hands and forearms out and up from the sides of the body in a circular motion. Step to the east into a right hand posture. As the left foot strikes the ground and the right foot pivots, the hands move into position blocking the face. Turn the left shoulder and trunk slightly sideways, presenting a smaller target than if the torso and shoulders were facing straight ahead (Figure B). If necessary, refer to page 37, Step 2 to review the circular motion for this block.

Figure C.

3. Pivot 180° to the west into a left hand posture (Figure C), moving the hands accordingly. Complete the hand movements and pivot at the same time. If necessary, refer to page 38, Step 3 to review the motion for this block.

4. Step to the south into a right hand posture (Figure D).

Figure D.

5. Pivot 180° to the north into a left hand posture (Figure E).

Figure E.

6. Step to the southwest into a right hand posture (Figure F).

Figure F.

Figure G.

7. Pivot 180° to the northeast, into a left hand posture (Figure G).

Figure H.

8. Step to the northwest into a right hand posture (Figure H).

Figure I.

9. Pivot 180° to the southeast into a left hand posture (Figure I).

Figure J.

Figure K.

Figure L.

10. Step with the left foot to the east into the home position, pivoting slightly on the right foot so the toes of both feet point forward, insides of the feet hip width apart. As the step is completed, move the arms so the wrists cross in front of the chest, keeping the left arm between the right arm and the body (Figure J). Continue a downward, circular motion, returning the hands to the sides, palms down, fingers pointed forward (Figure K).

This completes *Parting the Clouds* beginning with a right hand posture (to the right). To do the dance beginning with a left hand posture (to the left), merely reverse the hand and foot movements already explained.

To flow smoothly into the dance to the left direction after completing it to the right direction, immediately step into a left hand posture after Step 10 above. As the right foot strikes the ground and the left foot pivots, move the hands and forearms out and up in a circular motion from the sides of the body, blocking the face. Now perform the entire movement to the left direction, reversing the hand and foot movements explained for the right direction.

After blocking to the last corner (northeast), step with the right foot to the east into the home position, pivoting slightly on the left foot so the toes of both feet point forward, insides of the feet hip width apart. As the step is completed, move the arms so the wrists cross in front of the chest, keeping the right arm between the left arm and the body (Figure L). Continue a downward, circular motion, returning the hands to the sides, palms down, fingers pointed forward (Figure K).

Do *Parting the Clouds,* now a kilmo, slowly, art form, maintaining the flowing motion. Fighting form is done as fast as one can, still maintaining the flowing motion. Practice flowing smoothly from one posture to another without stops and without other mistakes in hand, foot, or body posture. Flow naturally without thinking. Relax. Open (begin) with *The Salutation.* Without stops, flow into the dance. Then close (end) with *The Salutation,* flowing smoothly from the last movement of the dance.

By flowing, the student will become aware of the physical, mental, and spiritual health benefits of all the Gohn Dagow movements.

Only after perfecting Parting the Clouds physically can it become a meditation. Imagine being a mythological dragon of ancient times, all-powerful, always alert and able to move swiftly and smoothly in any direction, constantly aware of everything about him. He is floating with his head and shoulders slightly above the clouds, flowing through them slowly, gracefully, brushing them aside without disturbing them. Do not merely intellectualize this situation, else the dance cannot be a meditation. Become the ancient dragon in the clouds, and be there throughout the entire dance. When this is done, the dance is truly Parting the Clouds.

CHAPTER III

Defending

The hand and arm movements of *Parting the Clouds* are revealed as blocks in the fighting form. However, practice this dance primarily in its art form as a meditation and as a means of learning to flow. *Parting the Clouds* is a means of learning physical and mental balance and control. It is also a means of improving health by relieving stress, head congestion, and headaches. The balance and control learned through this dance will aid the student in learning the techniques and drills that follow; for *how can one control an opponent, if one cannot control himself.*

Striving for and obtaining mental and physical control is traditionally part of the monk way. Practicing this philosophy of control is essential to Gohn Dagow in both its fighting and art form. However, if such control is possible, why fight? Again, the answer is in the philosophy of the *Yin-Yang*. If there is good in evil and vice versa, then there may be a time when defense is essential. Thus, *fight only in self-defense or to defend others; if fighting is necessary, fight with a sense of Truth, Justice, and Honor.*

Truth, justice, and honor are relative concepts, and finally the individual must define them himself. In Gohn Dagow there is a notion of justice that two philosophies convey. The philosophies are: *The Gift* and *The Three Degrees of Danger*. The philosophy of *The Gift* is: *If you accept a dishonorable gift, you honor the giver and dishonor yourself. If you do not accept the gift, you honor yourself, and the dishonor remains with the giver. However, if the gift is honorable, and you accept it, you honor yourself and the giver.*

The *Three Degrees of Danger* is:

1. *Verbal insults injure only the pride. Thus, ignore verbal insults, for accepting or returning them is dishonorable.*

2. *If attacked and physical harm is imminent, but life is not in danger, the student can justly defend himself with regard for life and limb.*

3. *If a student is attacked, and it is clear that the intent is to kill or permanently injure, the student may justly defend himself in any way available. However, if someone not in control of his senses threatens a student's life, the student must act accordingly.*

The mental and physical control and the sense of truth, justice, and honor in these philosophies help the Gohn Dagow student become more conscious of his own abilities and potential and more aware of his relationships with others.

In Gohn Dagow the philosophies, movement, and *chi*, the energy life force, are cirular. They are also all interrelated. When these elements are in perfect balance, physical, mental, and spiritual harmony is achieved. This balance and harmony can be accomplished with knowledge, skill and effort. These three factors comprise *The Three Circles of Life. The philosophy is:*

Effort is not equal to skill; Skill is not equal to knowledge; Only through knowledge and effort can skill be attained.

With this philosophy in mind, let us begin some of the techniques. Although *Parting the Clouds* and *The Salutation* are defense maneuvers, the following techniques apply more directly to fighting situations. However, some of them, too, can be meditations. Before learning any of the fighting techniques, the student must first learn an important blocking sequence used in many Gohn Dagow movements.

Circle Blocking - Closing *(Stationary)*

Circle Blocking is a blocking technique when used for self defense. As a moving meditation, its flowing, circular motions help the student discover the inner energy and control mentioned earlier. As a healing exercise it relieves stress, bursitis, tension, and muscle tightness in the shoulders.

Figure A.

1. Stand in the ready posture (Figure A).

Figure B.

2. Rotate the right hand so the palm faces forward. Keeping the right hand straight in line with the forearm, raise the right hand and forearm out and up from the right side of the body. Keep the elbow close to the body, but not tight against it (Figure B). Stop the right hand after it slightly passes the nose (Figure C). Fingertips of the right hand are above the eyebrows. This hand is blocking the face.

Figure C.

3. Rotate the left hand so the palm faces forward. Raise the left hand and forearm out and up from the left side of the body until the fingertips are at diaphragm height. Keep the elbow close to the body, but not tight against it (Figure B). Continue this circular motion across the midsection and down to the groin (Figure C). Stop the left hand at the groin palm facing down, fingers pointing to the right. This hand is blocking the groin.

4. Continue the circular motions of the right hand, moving it across and down the left side of the body (Figure D), stopping at the groin, palm down, blocking the groin (Figure E).

5. Continue the circular motion of the left hand, moving it past the left leg. Keep the palm down until after the left hand passes the left leg. Then rotate the left hand so the palm faces out. Keeping the left hand in line with the forearm, raise the left hand and forearm out and up from the left side of the body, stopping it slightly past the nose (Figures D and E). The left hand is now blocking the face.

6. To return to Figure C: circle the left hand down the right side of the body, stopping to block the groin; and circle the right hand out and up the right side of the body, stopping to block the face.

Figure D.

This completes the cycle for *Circle Blocking - Closing*. The hands move together in the circular motion as described above, forming intersecting circles. Practice until the movement becomes natural. If it is too difficult, circle the hands independently. Circle the right hand and forearm counter-clockwise, and circle the left hand and forearm clockwise; then put the two together. The movement is performed correctly when the hands circle simultaneously, one hand circling to block the face and the other circling to block the groin, smoothly, flowing, without stops. After learning *Circle Blocking* stationary, learn it walking.

Figure E.

Since *Circle Blocking* walking involves lower body movement as well as upper body movement, the rewards are greater for doing this movement walking than for doing it stationary; the rewards will be revealed internally to each individual.

Circle Blocking - Closing *(Walking)*

1. Stand in the ready posture (Figure A).

Figure A.

2. Step with the left foot into a comfortable stance. While stepping, *Circle Block* with the left hand to block the groin, and *Circle Block* with the right hand to block the face (Figure B). Refer to *Circle Blocking - Closing (Stationary)* page 48, if necessary. Both blocks are completed when the left foot strikes the ground (Figure B). This is a right hand posture.

Figure B.

3. Step with the right foot and at the same time *Circle Block* so the right hand is down, blocking the groin, and the left hand is up, blocking the face (Figure C). This is a left hand posture. Continue walking in a straight line, *Circle Blocking* until the movement becomes natural.

Figure C.

Short Arm One-Two *(Right Hand Posture)*

After learning *Circle Blocking* both stationary and walking, the student can learn the first drill normally taught in the classroom. It introduces the student to the push-pull action of the more advanced techniques, to projecting energy, to flowing motions. *The Short Arm One-Two* is relatively simple; but to learn and execute the movement properly, physical and mental control are essential.

Figure A.

1. Stand in the ready posture (Figure A).

Figure B.

2. Circle block with the left hand while drawing the right hand to the right side, palm up. At the same time, step forward with the left foot (Figures B and C). Be sure the blocking hand passes both the face, with the fingertips above the eyebrows, and the groin before returning it to the side palm up (Figure D).

Figure C.

3. Strike with a *Dragon's Head* with the right hand to the diaphragm of an opponent about the student's own height. Return the left hand to the left side palm up after the circle passes the groin (Figure D). The block, step, and strike occur simultaneously. The block with the left hand partially hides the strike. The formation of the *Dragon's Head* is shown below (Figure F).

Figure D.

Figure E.

4. Immediately after delivering the *Dragon's Head*, strike with the left *Heel Palm* to the face of the same opponent. At the same time, draw the right hand back to the right side, palm up (Figure E).

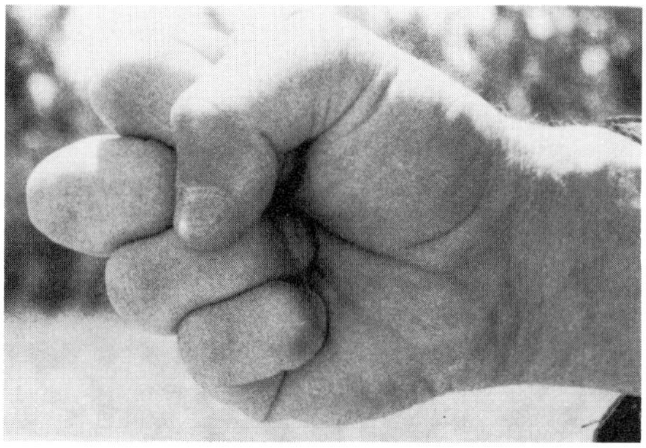

Figure F.

The *Heel Palm* is formed by flexing the back of the hand toward the forearm, thereby tightening the heel of the hand. The heel of the hand strikes the target (Figure G).

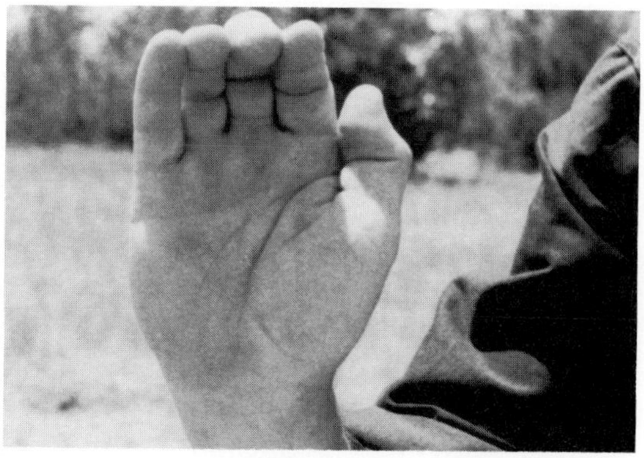

Figure G.

These two strikes occur one right after the other, simulating a push-pull action. The effect of pulling one arm in while thrusting out the other generates tremendous energy for each strike that is projected out the hands. Practice this drill from the ready posture, beginning first with the right hand and then with the left. It is important to return each hand to the side, palm up, before delivering each strike because the power for the strikes comes from the abdominals. Moreover, holding the palm up at the side demonstrates control. Be sure to twist the hand while delivering the strike, counterclockwise for the right hand and clockwise for the left. Do not form the hand posture while the hands are at the sides. Form them on the way to the target.

A strike is performed by thrusting the striking hand out to maximum extension but not locking the elbow. Relax the elbow slightly after the forearm reaches maximum extension, allowing the hand to snap back slightly.

Short Arm One-Two *(Left Hand Posture)*

1. Perform the *Short Arm One-Two* starting from a left hand posture merely by reversing the instructions given for starting from the right hand posture. The movements starting from the left hand posture will not be explained, but the illustrations should answer questions that might arise.

Figure A.

Figure B.

Figure C.

When the student can do the *Short Arm One-Two* smoothly in the stationary position, practice it walking. First, step with the left foot and *Circle Block* with the left hand, while delivering the *Dragon's Head* with the right hand and the *Heel Palm* with the left. Then step with the right foot and *Circle Block* with the right hand, while delivering the *Dragon's Head* with the left hand and the *Heel Palm* with the right. *Remember to block before the beginning of each sequence.* In the *Short Arm One-Two* the hand that strikes first in one sequence blocks for the next. Practice the drill until it can be done in the art form, slowly, smoothly, and without tension or mistakes. Then gradually increase speed to the fighting form, fast and smooth. This drill can also be done with tension for exercise and muscle tone.

Figure D.

It is important to stress that all the movements should be done slowly at first. The body needs to be warmed up before doing the techniques fast or with tension. If the body is not warmed up first, one could pull muscles, injure tendons, or dislocate joints. With the *Short Arm One-Two* the arms need strengthening to withstand the stress on the elbows.

Figure E.

The reason this is a short arm drill is because the left foot is forward when the right hand is striking, and the right foot is forward when the left hand is striking. Use this posture in close rather than for long-range situations. This technique is primarily done in the forward direction (advancing).

Long Arm One-Two *(Right Hand Posture)*

Another technique that offers somewhat more distance is the *Long Arm One-Two*. This movement has longer range than the *Short Arm One-Two* because the left foot is forward when the left hand is striking, and the right foot is forward when the right hand is striking.

Figure A.

1. Stand in the ready posture (Figure A).

Figure B.

2. *Circle Block* with the right hand. When starting the *Circle block*, step back one step with the right foot into a comfortable stance, drawing the left hand to the left side palm up (Figure B).

Figure C.

3. Continue the *Circle Block*, hiding the hand posture (Figure C).

4. As the right foot strikes the ground, deliver a *Panther* strike with the left hand to the neck of an opponent about the student's height (Figure D). (The *Panther* hand posture is shown below left). The right hand *Circle Block* has now passed the groin and returned to the right side, palm up. Do Figures B, C, and D as one movement. As the right foot strikes the ground, the left hand strikes, and the right hand returns to the side palm up with a push-pull action. The block, step, and strike are all done together.

5. Immediately after delivering the *Panther* strike, form a *Sleeping Ram* (vertical fist) with the right hand, and strike to the abdomen of the same opponent. At the same time, return the left hand to the side, palm up with a push-pull action (Figure E). (The *Sleeping Ram* hand posture is shown below right).

This is the complete cycle for the *Long Arm One-Two* stepping into the right hand posture. As with the *Short Arm One-Two*, the *Long Arm One-Two* employs the push-pull action, and it generates energy for each strike that comes from the abdominals and is projected out through the hands. Do not form the hand postures at the side before striking; form them as the arm delivers the technique. This avoids telegraphing them. Observe this rule for all hand postures.

It is also essential for one strike to follow immediately after the other. In effect, they are both done as one, just as in the *Short Arm One-Two*.

Figure D.

Figure E.

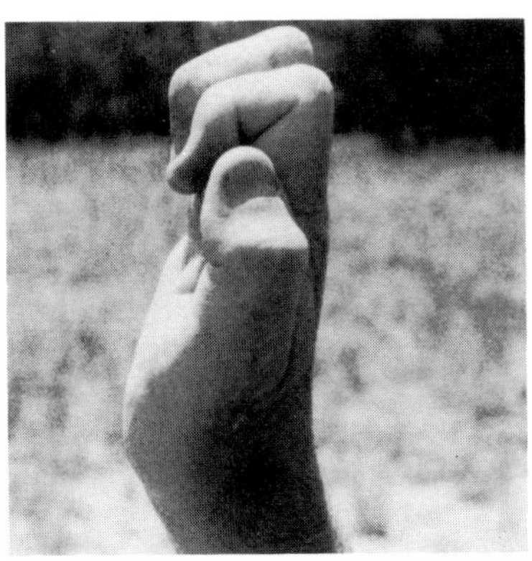

Long Arm One-Two *(Left Hand Posture)*

After learning the *Long Arm One-Two* stepping into the right hand posture, learn it stepping into the left hand posture.

Figure A.

1. Stand in the ready posture (Figure A).

Figure B.

2. *Circle Block* with the left hand. When starting the *Circle Block*, step back with the left foot into a comfortable stance, drawing the right hand to the right side, palm up (Figure B).

3. Continue to *Circle Block*, hiding the hand posture (Figure C).

Figure C.

4. As the left foot strikes the ground, deliver a *Panther* strike with the right hand to the neck of an opponent about the student's height (Figure D). The left hand *Circle Block* has now passed the groin and returned to the left side, palm up. Do Figures B, C, and D as one movement. As the left foot strikes the ground, the right hand strikes, and the left hand returns to the left side palm up with a push-pull action.

Figure D.

5. Immediately follow the *Panther* strike with a *Sleeping Ram* with the left hand. Draw the right hand back to the right side palm up with a push-pull action, while delivering the left hand strike (Figure E).

Figure E.

Just as in the *Short Arm One-Two*, the hand that delivers the first strike in the *Long Arm One-Two* blocks for the next sequence. Practice walking in a straight line, slowly, until the technique flows smoothly. Then increase speed to the fighting form. After the drill can be done slowly and fast, practice it slowly and fast with tension for exercise. As with the *Short Arm One-Two*, do the *Long Arm One-Two* stationary before doing it walking. The *Long Arm One-Two* is primarily done in the yielding direction.

The terms *short arm* and *long arm* have meanings other than those already explained. Short arm is usually used with *advancing*, and long arm is usually used with *yielding*. Advancing refers to forward movement, yielding refers to backward motion. Although the underlying philosophy in Gohn Dagow is *nothing is so permanent as never to change*, for the sake of continuity, instruction, and communication, short arm drills and techniques are generally done advancing, long arm yielding. The terms *advancing* and *yielding* are more appropriate than "charging" or "retreating," or "forward" and "backward." Moreover, the terms *advancing* and *yielding* represent the philosophies of movement more accurately than the terms "forward" and "backward."

The philosophy that *there is strength in yielding* is the primary reason for the specific terms. There can be a purpose in yielding, whether it is to prepare for an advance, utilize an opponent's momentum, or rest and gain strength. However, strength in yielding is effective only when one knows how far to yield.

竹與
橡樹

The Bamboo and the Oak

The bamboo yields under the weight of the winter
snow and springs back;
The oak, unyielding, breaks.

Snap Kick

After learning the two most basic hand techniques, the student should learn the two most basic foot techniques. Most martial arts books illustrate and explain the *Snap Kick.* Because this kick is basically the same in all forms, only a brief explanation of it is included here.

Figure A.

1. Stand with feet parallel, hands on hips (Figure A).

Figure B.

2. Spring off the ball of the left foot, raising the left leg so the thigh is parallel to the ground, toes pointed down (Figure B).

Figure C.

3. Kick straight out in front at least knee high, preferably higher, keeping the toes pointed (Figure C).

4. After kicking, return the left leg so the thigh is parallel to the ground (Figure D).

Figure D.

5. Return the left leg to the starting position (Figure E).

Figure E.

For self defense, the target for the *Snap Kick* is the area of the body from the diaphragm down. Practicing kicking as high as possible develops the power, speed, flexibility, and balance that are needed when the technique is used for self defense.

Snap Kick *(Advancing and Yielding)*

The *Snap Kick* should be done slowly at first. Be sure the legs are conditioned before doing this technique hard or fast. As it utilizes knee action, the muscles in the leg and tendons in the knee should be strong enough to withstand the stress of the kick when it is done fast.

Snap Kicking with the right leg is done the same way as *Snap Kicking* with the left leg. The kick can also be done from a "T" stance, a forward bow, a modified bow, or many other stances. The kick can be executed with either the forward or the rear leg, when *Snap Kicking* from any of the above stances (i.e. when the feet are not parallel). However, the forward leg, especially in formal dances, is most often used for *Snap Kicking*. The *Snap Kick* can also be done stationary, walking, advancing, or yielding. As this is a relatively simple technique, no illustrations will accompany this text.

Snap Kick *(Advancing)*

1. Stand in the ready posture.
2. Pivot on the center of the right foot while *Snap Kicking* to the front with the left foot. The body's weight should be centered over the right leg while kicking; the right knee should be slightly bent. Do not lean. Remain balanced.
3. After kicking, return the left leg to the position shown in Figure B, page 64.
4. Then, return the left foot to the ground a comfortable distance in front of and perpendicular to the right foot, forming a "T" stance (right hand posture). The body's weight is again equally distributed between both feet.
5. The posture is now created to *Snap Kick* to the front with the right foot in the same manner as with the left. The student advances as he alternately *Snap Kicks* with the left foot and right foot.

Snap Kick *(Yielding)*

1. Stand in the ready posture.
2. Take one step to the rear with the right foot, stepping into a right hand posture (feet only).
3. *Snap Kick* with the left foot. Again, the body's weight should be centered over the right leg; the right knee should be slightly bent. Do not lean. Remain balanced.
4. After kicking, return the left leg to the position shown in Figure B, page 64.
5. Return the left foot to the ground in front of and perpendicular to the right foot, reforming the right hand posture.
6. Then, take one step to the rear with the left foot, stepping into a left hand posture
7. *Snap Kick* with the right foot.
8. After kicking, return the right leg so the thigh is parallel to the ground, toes pointed down.
9. Now, return the right foot to the ground in front of and perpendicular to the left foot, reforming the left hand posture.

The student yields as he alternately *Snap Kicks* with the left and right foot. Notice that the rear leg is kicking while advancing, and the front leg is kicking while yielding.

Scoop Kick *(Right Leg)*

Another important kick is the *Scoop Kick.* It is only briefly explained here to reveal some of its "secrets."

Several different movements are combined with the *Scoop Kick.* The student will learn some of them in the following pages. From the most to the least difficult, they are: the *Scoop Kick Walk with Strikes*; the *Scoop Kick Walk with Circling Hands*; the *Scoop Kick Walk*; and the *Scoop Kick* itself. Before learning the first three techniques, the *Scoop Kick* alone must be learned.

Figure A.

1. Stand with hands on hips in a modified forward bow, weight centered between both feet, left foot in front of the right, left foot turned slightly to the right (Figure A).

Figure B.

2. Keeping the head and back straight, *Scoop Kick* with the right foot, kicking directly in front and as high as possible. Do not bend the knee, but do not lock it. The leg action is from the hip. Point the toes (Figure B).

3. Return to Figure A.

4. To do the *Scoop Kick* with the left leg, repeat Steps 1 and 2 above; (see Figures C and D and substitute movements for the left leg that were described for the right).

The *Scoop Kick* is executed differently from the *Snap Kick*. In the *Scoop Kick*, the kicking leg should be behind the forward leg. The "magic" of this movement is that the opponent should not see the kick, except perhaps just after impact.

Practice this kick as a warm-up exercise or as a drill, slowly or fast. When done at art form speed, the *Scoop Kick* is an excellent exercise for drawing energy into the lower back and hips, and for developing balance and control. It also relaxes and strengthens the muscles in the lower back. When the *Scoop Kick* is done fast, it builds endurance and strengthens muscles and tendons in the lower back and abdomen. Practice *Scoop Kicking* as high as possible to develop speed, power, and flexibility; but when used for self defense, the instep of the kicking foot strikes between the opponent's legs.

The *Scoop Kick* should be done slowly at first. As this movement comes primarily from the hip, that area must be conditioned before doing the kick hard or fast.

The student can also perform this technique, as well as many others, in the small space of a bedroom or living room. Always having a separate space to practice is not absolutely necessary. In ancient times monks who were captured by hostile war lords were incarcerated in small cells, released only to fight. Although space was limited, they could practice enough techniques to maintain a constant state of battle readiness. However, many monks were confined to body cages, where whole body movement was impossible. In such cases the monks relied on meditation as well as past experiences and training to keep them battle ready. Just as Confucious, according to tradition, mastered archery through meditation, the student can improve and perhaps perfect physical movements through meditation. So even if the student cannot always find space to practice, he can still perform all the movements mentally.

Figure C.

Figure D.

Scoop Kick Walking

After learning the *Scoop Kick* from the stationary position, learn it walking. Do the *Scoop Kick Walking* just as the *Scoop Kick Stationary*, except there is no need to return to the ready posture after each kick.

1. Stand in the ready posture. *Note:* No illustrations will accompany this explanation.

2. Step into a modified forward bow with the left foot.

3. *Scoop Kick* with the right foot.

4. Instead of returning the right foot to the starting position after the kick, take one step forward; that is, allow the right foot to return to the ground in front of the left after the kick. When the foot strikes the ground, it should strike on the ball of the foot first, rather than on the heel. The resulting posture is a modified forward bow, right foot in front, ready to *Scoop Kick* with the left foot. After *Scoop Kicking* with the left foot, allow it to return to the ground in front of the right; again, the ball of the foot strikes the ground first. The posture created now is the same as Step 2 above. Continue this procedure while walking in a straight line, alternately *Scoop Kicking* with the right and left legs.

Scoop Kick Walk with Circling Hands *(Circle Blocking)*

After learning the *Scoop Kick* and the *Scoop Kick Walk,* the student should learn the *Scoop Kick Walk with Circling Hands.* Refer to previous pages to review *Circle Blocking.*

Figure A.

1. From the ready posture step into a right hand modified forward bow, left foot forward. At the same time *Circle Block* so the left hand is down, the right hand up (Figure A).

Figure B.

2. *Scoop Kick* with the right leg, and at the same time *Circle Block* so the right hand is palm down on the inside of the right leg blocking the groin. The left hand is up blocking the face (Figure B) as the foot reaches its apex.

3. Instead of stepping out after kicking with the right foot, remain balanced on the left leg. Swing the right leg back parallel to the left, keeping it slightly off the ground. At the same time, *Circle Block* again so the left hand is down blocking the groin, and the right hand is up blocking the face (Figure C).

Figure C.

4. Take one step forward, touching the ball of the right foot to the ground first, in a smooth, gliding motion (Figure D). At the step, the right hand circles down to block the groin, the left circles up to block the face. The right foot is now forward in the modified bow, ready for the *Scoop Kick* with the left foot.

5. Since the posture is now created to *Scoop Kick* with the left foot, execute the *Scoop Kick* (Figure E). *Circle Block* so the right hand is up, blocking the face, and the left hand is palm down, blocking the groin.

6. Return the left foot parallel to the right, but slightly off the ground, balancing on the right foot. *Circle Block* so the right hand is palm down, blocking the groin, and the left hand is up, blocking the face (Figure F).

7. Take one step forward with the left foot, and at the same time *Circle Block* so the left hand is palm down, blocking the groin, and the right hand is up, blocking the face (Figure A). The posture is now the same as the starting posture (Figure A).

This is the full cycle of the *Scoop Kick Walk with Circling Hands.* Continue practicing in a straight line, alternately kicking with one leg then the other while *Circle Blocking.* First, do this movement stationary by returning to the ready posture after each step so kicking can be properly executed in the fighting form, art form slowly, or flowing and fast; then do it walking.

When done fast, the *Circle Blocking* phase of this technique is an excellent exercise for strengthening the muscles and thickening the tendons in the shoulders. When the strikes are added (next phase), the muscles and tendons are conditioned even more. The *Scoop Kick* phase conditions the lower back, as already mentioned on page 68. When done in the art form, *Circle Blocking* draws healing energy into the shoulders, upper back and chest; and it also relaxes muscles in those areas.

As a moving meditation, the entire movement balances the energy of the upper and lower body. The flowing motion centers and focuses the student.

Figure D.

Figure E.

Figure F.

Scoop Kick Walk with Strikes *(Right Leg Kicking)*

The next technique is the *Scoop Kick Walk with Strikes.* The foot movements for this technique are the same as those for the *Scoop Kick Walk with Circling Hands;* only the hand movements differ.

Figure A.

1. Stand in the ready posture (Figure A).

Figure B.

2. Step into a modified forward bow with the left foot, *Circle Blocking* as in the *Scoop Kick Walk,* left hand down, right up (Figure B).

Figure C.

3. As the *Scoop Kick* with the right foot begins, draw the left hand to the left side, palm up, preparatory to striking (Figure C).

4. Complete the *Scoop Kick* with the right leg. As the kick reaches its apex, execute a left *Heel Palm* to the face of an opponent about the student's own height (Figure D). The right hand circles down to block the groin. Be sure the left foot remains flat on the ground while kicking.

Figure D.

5. Swing the right leg back parallel to the left and slightly off the ground, as in the *Scoop Kick Walk*, and both hands *Circle Block* again so the right blocks the face and the left blocks the groin (Figure E).

Figure E.

6. Circle the right hand down to block the groin. Step forward into a modified forward bow with the right foot. Draw the left hand to the left side, palm up and then strike with another left *Heel Palm* to the face of the same opponent (Figure F).

Figure F.

Properly execute the *Heel Palm* strike by thrusting the hand out, rotating the palm as the arm moves out, completing the twist at the instant of maximum extension. However, do not lock the elbow. Relax the elbow slightly after the forearm reaches maximum extension. Allow the hand to snap back slightly, do not leave it stiffly out in front.

Correct timing is important. In Figure B, page 72, complete the circle blocks as the left foot strikes the ground. Both hands rotate at the same time. In Figure D, page 73, the right hand circles, the right foot reaches its maximum height, and the left *Heel Palm* are all delivered at the same time. In Figure F, page 73, *Circle Block* with the right hand, step into the modified forward bow with the right foot, and complete the left *Heel Palm* strike all at the same time also. Hands and feet all move together at a uniform pace so the entire movement flows as one.

Scoop Kick Walk with Strikes *(Left Leg Kicking)*

After Figure F, page 73, the posture is created to perform the *Scoop Kick Walk with Strikes* with the left foot kicking first.

Figure G.

1. From Figure F, page 73, *Scoop Kick* with the left foot. Draw the right hand to the right side, palm up and deliver a right *Heel Palm* to the face of the opponent. At the same time *Circle Block* to the groin with the left hand (Figure G). Be sure the right foot remains flat on the ground.

Figure H.

2. Allow the left leg to swing back parallel to the right, slightly off the ground, and *Circle Block* so the right hand blocks the groin, and the left hand blocks the face (Figure H).

Figure I.

3. Circle the left hand down to block the groin. Step forward into a modified forward bow with the left foot. Draw the right hand to the right side, palm up, and strike with another right *Heel Palm* to the face of the same opponent (Figure I).

This completes the cycle for the *Scoop Kick Walk with Strikes*. Remember: deliver the strikes in this technique from the side; that is, draw the hands to the sides before striking (Figure C, page 72). As with the other techniques, practice this one slowly at first, gradually increasing speed to the fighting form.

Scoop Kick, Knee, Spears *(Right Hand Posture)*

Before leaving the *Scoop Kick,* there are two more useful drills based on the *Scoop Kick* that the beginning student should learn; they are the *Scoop Kick, Knee, Spears,* and the *One-Two, Scoop Kick, Knee, Spears.* Since the latter is more difficult, the former will be learned first.

1. Stand in the ready posture (Figure A).

Figure A.

2. Step into a modified forward bow with the left foot. *Circle Block* so the left hand blocks the groin, and the right hand blocks the face (Figure B).

Figure B.

3. *Scoop Kick* with the right foot and *Circle Block* with both hands so the right hand blocks the groin, and the left hand blocks the face (Figure C). Be sure the left foot remains flat on the ground during the kick.

Figure C.

4. Allow the right foot to return naturally to the ground in front of the left after the kick. It should return to the ground in another modified forward bow. As the right foot strikes the ground (ball of the foot first), cross block with the left wrist over the right (Figure D). Be sure to keep the fingers together, and extend the hands slightly beyond the right knee.

Figure D.

Figure E.

5. Immediately after the right foot strikes the ground, spring off the ball of the left foot, raising the left thigh parallel to the ground at least hip high, toes pointed down. Both hands and arms circle out from the sides of the body, and the hands then pull the head of the opponent into the rising knee (Figures E, F, G, and H). As the knee reaches its maximum height, the hands and arms complete their circular motion and slap the knee, simulating the impact of the *Knee Lift* to the face of the opponent.

Figure F.

6. While returning the left foot to the ground and parallel to the right, form two *Spears*. As the left foot strikes the ground, thrust the *Spears* forward into the opponent's groin, bending the knees with the *Spear* thrust (Figures I and J). See Figures I and J for the *Spear* hand posture.

This completes the cycle for the *Scoop Kick, Knee, Spears*. Repeat the drill *Scoop Kicking* with the left leg first. The cycle for the *Scoop Kick, Knee, Spears,* stepping into the left hand posture, is shown on page 79. Practice walking in a straight line, alternating hands and feet, as explained. As with the other drills, do this one art form and fighting form.

When done art form, the *Knee Lift* in this drill in excellent for drawing energy into the hips. It limbers the hip joints and muscles, relieves pain in the hips and lower back, and increases flexibility in those areas.

Figure H.

Figure I.

Figure G.

Figure J.

Scoop Kick, Knee, Spears *(Left Hand Posture)*

No text will accompany the pictures for *Scoop Kick, Knee, Spears* from a Left Hand posture, since those instructions are merely opposite those already explained for the Right Hand Posture.

Figure A.

Figure B.

Figure C.

Figure D.

Figure E.

Figure F.

Figure G.

Figure H.

山
雪
草

Mountain - Snow/Grass

*The mountain is beautiful
when covered with snow,
but when the snow melts
the grass grows and
the mountain turns green.*

Short Arm One-Two, Scoop Kick, Knee, Spears *(Right Hand Posture)*

After learning the *Scoop Kick, Knee, Spears*, the *Short Arm One-Two,* learned earlier, can be added to it. Only minimal explanation will accompany the photos for this technique, as both parts have already been learned. The student only needs to combine the *Short Arm One-Two* with the *Scoop Kick, Knee, Spears* to execute the entire technique.

Figure A.

1. Stand in the ready posture (Figure A).

Figure B.

2. Execute the *Short Arm One-Two* (Figures B and C).

Figure C.

3. Circle the left hand down to block the groin and circle the right hand up to block the face. Simultaneously execute the *Scoop Kick* with the right leg (Figure D). Notice the *left* hand is blocking the groin and the *right* hand is blocking the face.

Figure D.

4. Perform the cross block after the *Scoop Kick*, extending crossed hands slightly in front of the knee (Figure E).

Figure E.

5. Execute the *Knee Lift* (Figures F through I).

Figure F.

Figure G.

Figure H.

Figure I.

Figure J.

Figure K.

6. Execute the *Spears* (Figures J and K).

Snap Kick, Heel Palm, Elbow *(Right Hand Posture)*

Just as the *Scoop Kick* was combined with other techniques, so can the *Snap Kick.* Two of the most commonly taught techniques that use the *Snap Kick* are the *Snap Kick, Heel Palm, Elbow* and the *Long Arm One-Two, Snap Kick, Heel Palm, Elbow.* The first movement mentioned will be learned first, as it is the easiest. However, the addition of extra techniques does not create a formal, classical dance that is opened and closed with *The Salutation.* Just as the *Short Arm One-Two, Scoop Kick, Knee, Spears* is not a formal dance but only a drill named for each technique within it, the movements added to the *Snap Kick* that the student is about to learn are only drills named for each technique within them.

Figure A.

The Snap Kick, Heel Palm, Elbow is the first technique of the two the student will now learn. Since the *Snap Kick* and the *Heel Palm* have already been explained, the *Elbow* is the only new movement in this technique. It will be explained as part of the entire movement.

Figure B.

1. Stand in the ready posture (Figure A).

2. Take one step to the rear with the right foot, and shift weight somewhat to the rear leg. Raise the left knee so the thigh is parallel to the ground, preparing for the *Snap Kick.* Draw the right hand to the right side palm up. At the same time, move the left hand vertically in front of the torso in a vertical block (Figure B).

3. When the vertical block is above the head, *Snap Kick* with the left foot (Figure C).

Figure C.

4. After the kick, allow the left foot to return to the ground naturally, a comfortable distance in front of the right. As the left foot strikes the ground, deliver a right *Heel Palm* to the face of the opponent, and at the same time, draw the left hand to the left side palm up (Figure D).

Figure D.

5. Strike with the left *Elbow* to the head of the same opponent, forcefully hitting the right hand (Figure E), simulating impact of the head against the elbow. When executing an *Elbow Strike*, be sure to keep the upper arm parallel to the ground. Strike with the bone of the elbow, not with the forearm.

Figure E.

6. Circle the left hand down to block the groin, and circle the right hand up to block the face (Figure F).

Figure F.

Snap Kick, Heel Palm, Elbow *(Left Hand Posture)*

Here are photos illustrating the *Snap Kick, Heel Palm, Elbow* stepping into a left hand posture, with the ready posture omitted. As with the other drills, do the *Snap Kick, Heel Palm, Elbow* first in its art form, then progress to fighting speed.

Figure A.

Figure B.

Figure C.

Figure D.

Figure E.

Long Arm One-Two, Snap Kick, Heel Palm, Elbow *(Right Hand Posture)*

After the student is proficient with the *Snap Kick, Heel Palm, Elbow,* he may add the *Long Arm One-Two* to the movement. The *Long Arm One-Two* has already been learned. To perform the *Long Arm One-Two, Snap Kick, Heel Palm, Elbow* all as one movement, the student needs only to combine the movements. Thus, little explanation will accompany the photos.

Remember to *Circle Block* with the right hand while stepping to the rear with the right foot into the right hand posture and delivering the *Panther* in the *Long Arm One-Two.*

The student can do both the *Snap Kick, Heel Palm, Elbow* and the *Long Arm One-Two, Snap Kick, Heel Palm, Elbow* stepping into the right or left hand posture. Indeed the student should learn both movements from both postures. The student should do the movements in the art form, slow and flowing, and the fighting form, fast and flowing.

Figure A.

Figure B.

Figure C.

Figure D.

Figure E.

Figure F.

CHAPTER IV

Three Circles of Life: Knowledge, Skill, and Effort

Up to this point the student has been primarily learning kicks. Although some hand postures were learned, they were not emphasized. The kicks have been developing balance and coordination, and toning muscles. However, kicks are not as versatile, martially, as hands. They do not exemplify the flowing motions so integral to Gohn Dagow. They do not provide the best means for contacting the inner energy.

Hands are better suited for performing flowing motions and helping the student contact his inner energy; they are also important weapons.

In Gohn Dagow, *the hands are the most important body weapons because their use is virtually unlimited.* The stature of the people who used Gohn Dagow centuries ago and the terrain where they used it were two main reasons the people so highly emphasized hand techniques. The southern Chinese were characteristically shorter than the northern Chinese. Thus, they needed a defense form that adapted well to close-range fighting. On the other hand, northern styles emphasized kicks and long-range techniques. Also, people in the South were more agrarian than those in the North. If fighting broke out in marshes or flooded rice paddies, kicking was difficult. Moreover, the use of hands is almost limitless, compared to the limitations of the feet.

Hand techniques are not just valuable fighting tools. For centuries people performed the *Hand Flower*, the first technique to be learned in this section, to help prevent and relieve the discomfort of arthritis in the hands. Moving the hands and fingers brings energy to the inflamed area, strengthens the muscles, and lubricates the joints. Painters and sculptors also used this technique to sensitize their hands before creating their art work.

Several hand postures have already been learned. The *Dragon's Head* and the *Heel Palm* were learned in the *Short Arm One-Two*. The *Panther* and the *Sleeping Ram* were learned in the *Long Arm One-Two*. These four hand postures are also part of the *Hand Flower*, a concise, unified statement of seven basic hand postures that opens and closes similarly to the formal dances. However, since the *Hand Flower* is only a hand movement, the feet are not involved in the opening or closing.

Hand Flower

According to oral tradition, a monk patterned the *Hand Flower* after observing the opening and closing of a flower. This is a beautiful movement because of its symbolism and because each posture has a history and tradition. Each movement imitates an object or an animal in nature.

Figure A.

1. To open the hand movement, the hands are in the same position as in *The Salutation (Figure A).*

Figure B.

2. Separate the hands about ten inches, keeping the fingers extended and joined with the thumb touching the edge of the hand (Figure B). This hand posture is called the *Sword.* When used as a fighting posture, either the point of the *Sword* (the fingers) or the edge or blade of the *Sword* (the edge of the hand) is the striking surface.

Figure C.

3. Keeping the hands the same distance apart, merely curl the fingers in the manner shown (Figure C). This hand posture is called the *Panther.* The point of the knuckles is the striking surface.

4. Keeping the hands the same distance apart, rotate the palms out and down, and spread the thumb away from the edge of the hand slightly. This hand posture is called the *Tree of Life*. The striking surface is the webbing between the thumb and forefinger.

Figure D.

5. Leaving the hands the same distance apart, move the ring finger of each hand to touch the thumb of each hand (Figure E). Slightly bend the index and middle finger of each hand, and separate them as shown. The little finger of each hand should be along side the ring finger of each hand. This is called the *Twin Dragon Seeking the Pearl of Life*. The striking portion of this hand posture is the tips of the index finger and forefinger.

Figure E.

6. Leaving the hands the same distance apart, curl the middle finger between the index and ring fingers so the knuckle protrudes slightly, ensuring that the middle finger is supported by both the fingers on each side and by the thumb underneath (Figure F). This hand posture is called the *Dragon's Head*. The striking portion of this hand posture is the knuckle of the middle finger. This hand posture was already learned in the *Short Arm One-Two*.

Figure F.

7. Keeping the hands the same distance apart, rotate the hands out, and at the same time move the middle finger (which is still curled) further into the hand, forming a fist, as shown (Figure G). Rotation stops when the hands are vertical. This hand posture is called the *Sleeping Ram* or *Vertical Fist.* The striking area is the knuckles of the fist or the entire front surface of the fist. This hand posture was also learned earlier in the *Long Arm One-Two.*

Figure G.

8. Leaving the hands the same distance apart, rotate both hands so the fingers point slightly up. Keep the fingers joined; bend them slightly. Flex the back of the hand toward the forearm, thereby tightening the heel of the hand (Figure H). This hand posture is called the *Heel Palm.* The striking surface is the heel of the hand. This hand posture was also learned earlier in the *Short Arm One-Two.*

Figure H.

9. Close the movement by bringing the hands back to the starting position (Figure I).

Figure I.

Practice the *Hand Flower* slowly at first, art form speed. The student should meditate on a flower opening and closing, and experience the resulting energy flow. Once the student can do the *Hand Flower* slowly and smoothly, increase the speed to fighting form. When done fast, the movement should be completed in less than a breath. Repeating the *Hand Flower* several times at a fast speed will help develop strength in the hands, wrists, and forearms.

Several techniques in the *Hand Flower* can be extremely dangerous. If a student ever uses them in self defense, he should exercise maximum caution and control, as with all Gohn Dagow movements. When performing the techniques in this book with the *Sword, Panther, Dragon's Head,* and *Sleeping Ram*, whether in practice or in self defense, keep the back of the hand in line with the wrist and forearm. The wrist should not be bent. If a student achieves a forceful impact with any of these four hand postures when the wrist is bent, it could break or sprain the wrist or hand.

The *Sword*, the *Tree of Life*, and the *Twin Dragon* are very dangerous techniques because they are primarily directed at vital areas. They should be used with maximum caution and control. When striking with the *Sword,* do not lock the fingers; keep them straight. When striking with the *Twin Dragon,* allow the wrist to move freely, as this is a wrist-flicking movement. When striking, the wrist propels the fingers forward, projecting them out, striking the target. Return them to the starting position with the reverse wrist action.

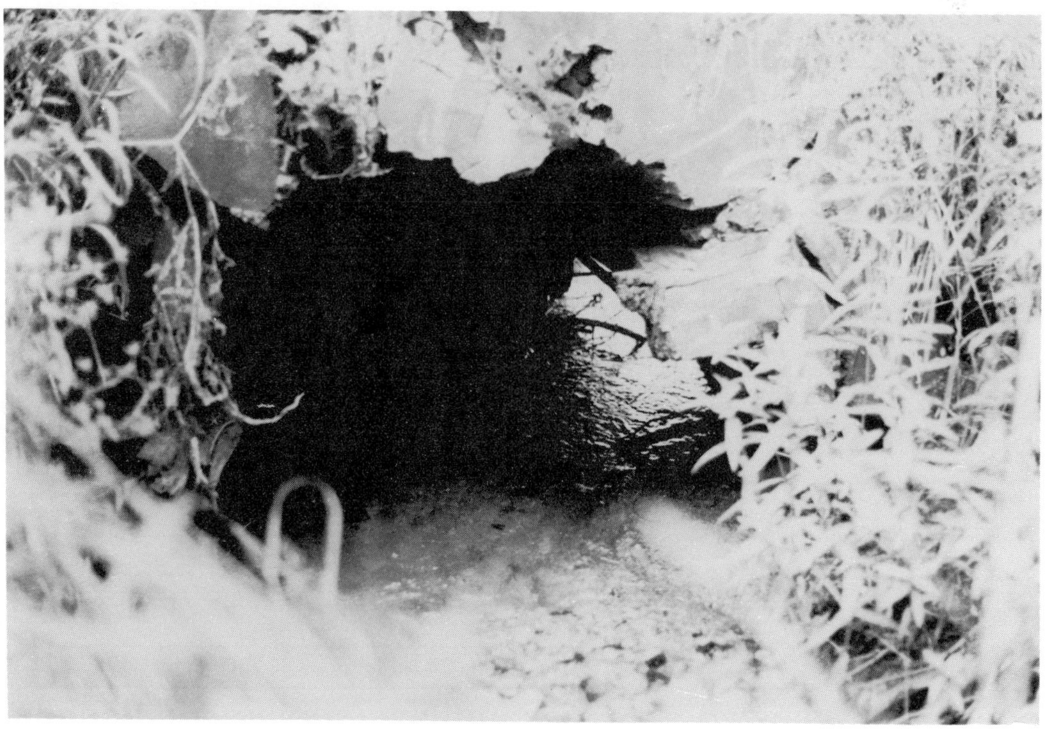

Stationary Ten *(Directions of the Ten Winds)*

The Stationary Ten is another movement that compliments the *Hand Flower* both physically and as an energy flow. It releases energy blocks. It balances the breath and circulation, energizes the circulatory system, and cleanses the respiratory system. It is excellent for relieving nasal congestion.

The Stationary Ten primarily involves the hands and arms. Do the *Stationary Ten* between sets of strenuous drills as a breathing exercise. The *Stationary Ten* is also called the *Directions of the Ten Winds,* because the movement includes all ten directions from which one may attack or defend.

Figure A.

1. Open with *The Salutation* (Figure A).

Figure B.

2. Continue the circular motion, separating the hands downward. As the hands pass the legs, rotate the hands so the palms face forward, fingers pointing down. Continue to raise the hands and forearms out and up from the sides of the body as in *The Salutation.* As the hands reach shoulder level, form a *Twin Dragon* with each hand. Crossing right hand over left, deliver the technique to the left and right corners (Figure B). They should be at eye level of an imagined opponent.

Figure C.

3. Form a *Sword* with each hand, palms down, and move the arms out to the sides, shoulder high (Figure C).

4. Rotate the palms up, keeping the *Sword* hand posture. Bring the hands and arms back to the center of the body, chest high (Figure D).

Figure D.

5. Maintain the *Sword* hand posture, palms up. Keeping the elbows into the sides, move them to the rear, chest high (Figure E).

Figure E.

6. Form a *Panther* hand posture with each hand, and deliver the technique to the front, neck high (Figure F).

Figure F.

7. Bend the wrists sharply, flexing the forearm, and allowing the fingers to separate and extend down. Rake the hands back toward and into the chest, keeping the elbows in (Figure G).

Figure H.

8. Rotate the palms up and extend the hands and arms overhead, straight above the shoulder, moving in line with the ears (Figure H).

9. After extending the arms overhead, form a fist with each hand. Bring the hands down in line with the ears, and tuck them into the armpits (Figures I and J).

Figure I.

Figure G.

Figure J.

10. Thrust the fists to the ground with a squat. Both feet should remain flat in the squat (Figure K).

11. Stand, and allow the fingers to straighten while standing (Figure L).

12. Close with *The Salutation* (Figure M).

Figure K.

Figure L.

Figure M.

The *Stationary Ten* is done primarily from the stationary position. Perform it slowly and smoothly, exemplifying the flowing motion; or do it fast. The student can also do it hard with tension for exercise.

When the *Stationary Ten* is done slowly and smoothly, it is an excellent breathing exercise. Coordinate the breathing with the hand and arm movements by first taking a deep breath through the nose, then exhale through the mouth while performing the *Twin Dragon.* Inhale through the nose with the *Swords*, palm down, and stretch the arms way out so the shoulder blades touch. Exhale through the mouth as the hands return to center. Inhale through the nose when moving the elbows to the rear. Exhale through the mouth with the *Panther.* Inhale with the *Rake.* Exhale through the mouth with the *Hand Palms* as shown in the photo. The energy comes out the center of the palm rather than the heel of the palm. Inhale through the nose while bringing the hands under the armpits and thrusting to the ground with the squat. Exhale when standing and returning to the ready posture, slowly opening the fists while rising.

Do this sequence slowly. While rising from the squat, open the fists and face the palms toward the body, finishing in the ready posture. Feel a tremendous surge of energy in the head, hands, arms, and the entire body. For centuries, this surge of energy achieved by performing the *Stationary Ten* and other movements has been called *"chi"* or inner energy. The *chi* is both a mental and a physical phenomenon. The student can contact the *chi* through either a physical or mental process, or both. Performing this movement creates much more than merely a physiological reaction. There is a sense of lightness and well-being, of peace, harmony, and joy. A complete discussion of *chi* is not intended here, but if the student performs the above movements as indicated, he should experience a more significant contact with his inner energy than he may have felt in *Parting the Clouds* and some of the other movements.

The *Stationary Ten, Hand Flower*, and *Parting the Clouds* can all be done in one unified kilmo as a meditation. When these kilmos are combined, they also form a meaningful exercise in flowing motion, and they are a means of tapping the inner energy. When combining the three kilmos into one continuous movement, it is important to perform *Parting the Clouds* first, then the *Hand Flower*, and the *Stationary Ten* last. It is also important to do the movements art form, slowly and smoothly, without any stops or jerks.

塘中的

漣漪

Ripples in the Pond

Just as ripples emanate from a pebble thrown into the center of a pond, so good deeds emanate and multiply from us.

Long Low *(Posture Only)*

After learning the hand postures, the student can learn a more complicated and strenuous technique: the *Long Low with Three Hands.* It is a variation of the *Scoop Kick* performed from a low posture; and it combines hands with a kick.

Before learning the entire movement, it is wise to first practice and become accustomed to the posture. Many people find the posture physically tiring and awkward for balance.

1. From the ready posture, step way out to the right side with the right foot, forming a "T" stance with the right foot perpendicular to the left (Figure A). Keep the left leg straight, but do not lock the knee. Keep the right thigh parallel to the ground. Both feet should be perfectly flat on the ground. Flexibility in the ankle is essential here, and it may be somewhat uncomfortable at first.

Figure A.

2. To perform the *Long Low* from the left hand posture, merely pivot on the centers of both feet 180° to the left, shifting the weight to the left leg so the left thigh is parallel to the ground and the right leg is straight. The torso should remain upright but not stiff, and the hands should remain on the hips (Figure B).

Figure B.

Practice this posture until it becomes comfortable. Do at least ten repetitions with each leg; then move into a right or left hand ready posture from the *Long Low.* It is essential to move swiftly, smoothly, and with balance from this *Long Low* stance to a ready posture. If balance is lost moving out of it in a real situation, the student would be at a disadvantage. Thus, practice assuming the stance and moving out of it.

After the student gains balance in the *Long Low,* and after it becomes comfortable and easy to move into a ready posture, add the *Three Hands.*

Long Low with Three Hands *(Right Hand Posture)*

1. From the ready posture, step to the left with the left foot into a right hand *Long Low* posture. At the same time, cross block with the right hand and forearm. Perform the cross block by moving the right hand and forearm from the shoulder, across the chest from right to left, blocking the face. Fingertips are above the eyebrows. Palm of the right hand is facing to the left. Keep the forearm as vertical as possible. Simultaneously form a fist with the left hand, and move it to the upper abdominal area (Figure A) in preparation for a strike.

Figure A.

2. After cross blocking, and without stopping, flow immediately into a diagonal, overhead block with the right hand and forearm (Figure B), fingers extended and joined. Perform the diagonal, overhead block merely by raising the forearm over the head, blocking the head (Figure B).

Figure B.

3. While completing the diagonal, overhead block, begin moving the left fist out and forward in an arc aimed at the testes of an opponent about the student's own height (Figure C). Bend the left arm slightly at the elbow at the start of the arc (Figures A and B). As the left fist moves forward toward its target, begin circling the right arm from the shoulder, back, down, and around the outside of the right leg (Figures B and C). The right elbow is slightly bent. Keep the right leg straight out behind as the left fist strikes the target (Figure C). The motion of the circling arms is now and will continue to be throughout this movement, a windmill motion from the shoulder.

Figure C.

4. After delivering the fist, continue the same circular motion, circling the left hand and arm up and the right hand and arm around toward the front (Figure D). Keep the fingers of the right hand extended and joined.

Figure D.

5. Continue the same circular motion of both arms. As the left arm is parallel to the right leg, the right hand delivers a *Heel Palm* to the face of an opponent who would be bent over after the first strike (Figure E). The momentum for the right *Heel Palm* begins in (Figure B), and it builds as the circular motion continues until impact in (Figure E). Notice that in this technique, none of the strikes come from the sides, as in the *Short Arm One-Two* and the *Long Arm One-Two*.

Figure E.

6. After the *Heel Palm* strike, the right hand continues circling up, around, back, and down to its position in Figure F. As it approaches maximum arc to the rear, the left hand comes from its position in Figure E, and forms a *Finger Thrust* that is thrust into the opponent's eyes. At the same time, a *Scoop Kick* is executed with the right leg, kicking with the instep between the opponent's legs (Figure F).

Figure F.

7. After *Scoop Kicking*, return the right foot to the ground in front of the left, while stepping out into the *Long Low* posture (Figure G). As the right foot strikes the ground, execute a left *Heel Palm*, starting from the height of its arc (Figure F), driving it in a circular motion down toward the ground. Notice the circular motion is now moving forward and down in an arcing motion toward the ground, not up and back. The point of impact for this *Heel Palm* is on the back of the head, neck, or torso of the opponent (Figure G).

Figure G.

8. As the left *Heel Palm* finishes, circle the right hand forward over the head, and toward the ground. Notice the circular motion of the right hand is also reversed at this point, similar to that of the left in Step 7 above. It, too, delivers a *Heel Palm* at the same point the left *Heel Palm* was delivered (Figure G). Continue circling the left hand down toward the ground and back while delivering the right *Heel Palm* (Figure H).

Figure H.

9. While delivering the right *Heel Palm* (Figure H), begin circling the left hand and arm forward, up, over the head and toward the ground. It delivers another *Heel Palm* at the same point as before (refer to Figure G). Immediately after delivering the *Heel Palm,* the left hand cross blocks across the face and then executes an overhead diagonal block. Then the right hand moves to block the groin and prepares to repeat the cycle, starting with the right fist (Figure I).

Figure I.

Long Low with Three Hands *(Left Hand Posture)*

To perform the *Long Low with Three Hands* by stepping into a left hand posture, merely substitute the left hand motions for the right hand motions and the right hand motions for the left hand motions already explained. After Step 9, page 108, the student is in the posture to do the *Long Low with Three Hands* from the left hand posture, beginning with a right hand fist. However, this is a difficult technique, and below is the sequence of the *Long Low with Three Hands* stepping into a left hand posture, although the verbal explanation is excluded.

Figure A.

Figure B.

Figure C.

As with all the other movements discussed, master the *Long Low with Three Hands* art form first; then practice it at fighting speed. The drill is excellent for developing the leg and lower back muscles. Because it involves circling the arms, it offers the same benefits of the *Circle Blocking* techniques for relieving tension and muscle tightness in the shoulders. It draws healing energy into the shoulders and lower back and gives them flexibility. It also strengthens and limbers the muscles and relieves pain and tension in the upper back. As a meditation, it circulates energy out from the body, releasing energy blocks and opening the channels for energy flow, while simultaneously focusing and centering the energy in the abdominals.

Figure D.

Figure E.

Figure F.

Figure G.

Figure H.

Right Side

Two additional techniques that will be discussed preparatory to explaining the formal kilmo with which the book will end are *Right Side* and *Left Side*. These movements also contain blocks, strikes, and kicks, but they are not formal dances themselves. They are only drills, but they exist as part of the formal drill that follows.

1. Stand in the ready posture facing east (Figure A).
2. Keeping the left arm straight, move the left hand and arm from the shoulder forward until the little finger is slightly in front of the left leg, palm facing to the right. Then, keeping the left arm straight, move the left hand and arm from the shoulder so the left hand passes the groin, executing a palm block.
3. As the left hand performs the movement described in Step 2 above, *Circle Block* with the right hand to block the face.
4. After the left hand passes the groin, rotate the left hand so the palm faces down (Figure B). Then circle the left hand and forearm up the right side of the body and past the face (Figures C and D). As the left hand and forearm begin to circle up the right side of the body, rotate the left hand so the palm faces forward (Figures C and D).
5. As the left hand performs the movement described in Step 4 above, the right hand and forearm continue their *Circle Block* down the left side of the body. They continue circling down to block the groin, palm down. Then the right hand is drawn to the right side, palm up, after it passes the groin (Figure C).
6. As the left hand block passes the face, step with the right foot to the southeast, and deliver a right *Heel Palm* to the floating ribs of an opponent the student's height (Figure D). *IMPORTANT: Do not drop the left block!*

Figure A.

Figure B.

Figure C.

7. Since the left arm is up after the block, use it for another strike. Form a *Heel Palm* with the left hand and strike to the head of the same opponent. At the same time, cock the left foot and draw the right hand to the right side palm up (Figure E). Remember, with a strike, the hand is withdrawn slightly (re-cocked) after the strike so it is ready for another strike. Strike with the left hand and draw the right to the side in a push-pull action.

8. *Side Snap Kick* with the edge of the left foot to the opponent's knee. *Circle Block* down with the left hand to block the groin, and *Circle Block* with the right hand to block the face (Figure F).

9. After the kick, step back with the left foot, placing it behind the right in a comfortable stance. Drag the right foot slightly toward the left. With the step, *Circle Block* with both hands, blocking the groin with the right, and blocking the face with the left (Figure G).

This completes the cycle for *Right Side.* Practice art form, gradually increasing speed to the fighting form. As with the other drills, do this movement with tension after learning it slowly and fast. The student can also do this movement stationary as well as walking.

Figure D.

Figure E.

Figure F.

Figure G.

Left Side

After completing the cycle for *Right Side*, the student is in position for *Left Side*. Because the two are so much alike, no explanation will accompany the photos for *Left Side*. Refer to the explanation of *Right Side* and merely substitute the left hand movements for the right, and substitute the right hand movements for the left.

Figure A.

Figure B.

Figure C.

Figure D.

Figure E.

Now that the full cycles for *Right Side* and *Left Side* have been presented, the student can practice them separately until he can do them in the fighting form, flowing and fast, as well as art form, flowing very slowly. Then the student can combine the movements and do them while advancing in a straight line. If the student has practiced the material presented thus far, there should be sufficient knowledge and skill to learn the last movement; for little can be accomplished without knowledge, skill, and effort.

Up and Back

The name of the formal fighting drill is the *Up and Back*, which begins with *Right Side* and *Left Side*. The *Up and Back* combines many of the preceding techniques. Although this is a short fighting drill, it is a formal drill. Thus, it opens and closes with *The Salutation.*

Figure A.

1. Perform *The Salutation* (Figures A and B).

Figure B.

2. The first technique is the *Right Side*, just learned (Figures C through H).

Figure C.

Figure D.

Figure E.

Figure F.

Figure G.

Figure H.

3. The next technique is *Left Side*, also just learned (Figures I through L).

Figure J.

Figure I.

Figure K.

Figure L.

4. Take two steps forward, while circle blocking (Figures M through N).

Figure M.

Figure N.

5. The next technique is the *Scoop Kick, Knee, Spears* (Figures O through R).

Figure P.

Figure O.

Figure Q.

Figure R.

6. Take three steps to the rear, while circle blocking (Figures S through U).

Figure S.

Figure T.

Figure U.

7. The next technique is the *Snap Kick, Heel Palm, Elbow* (Figures V through Y).

Figure V.

Figure W.

Figure X.

Figure Y.

Figure Z.

8. *Circle Block* while stepping to the rear with the left foot (Figure Z).

9. Cross block with the left hand over the right while stepping back with the right foot so the right foot is parallel to the left (Figure AA).

10. Close with *The Salutation* (Figures BB and CC).

Figure AA.

As with all the movements, the *Up and Back* is mental, physical, and spiritual. The mental, as always, is the most evident when first learning the movement It is then that concentration is highest. However, once the student knows the drill, he should flow with the movement, practicing it art form. Once the *Up and Back* is learned art form, the student should practice it fighting form; then, the physical aspect is most obvious. One physical experience that can occur is feeling tremendous surges of energy while performing this movement and many of the movements. Later, the student can learn to control and direct that energy. When the *Up and Back* can be done without thinking, the student can meditate on the movement while performing it, or he may even meditate on other things while doing the drill art form or fighting form. The student may also empty his mind and meditate while doing the movement. It is through the meditation that the student may experience spiritual changes that may result from practicing the art physically. A sense of peace and inner harmony should then be obvious.

Figure BB.

Figure CC.

CONCLUSION

Yin and Yang

Physical changes may bring about spiritual changes, just as spiritual changes bring about physical changes. Mastering the physical effects the spiritual. These are two philosophies that the serious student of the art will eventually encounter, and they should be mentioned to the prospective serious student as well. They are intrinsically linked to the surging energy felt during the physical movements.

Combining the physical with the spiritual provides the basis for the art. Gohn Dagow is designed for total individual development. It is through the spiritual aspect of the art that one can see the reality of the philosophy: *mind, body, and spirit are one.*

Let us reflect on some of the movements learned, and explain their spiritual dimension.

Parting the Clouds, the *Stationary Ten*, and the *Hand Flower* are three basic movements through which the student can feel the overwhelming surge of energy. But it must be emphasized that the awareness of the energy flow, achieved by being in a meditative state while performing the movements, is difficult to sense until the movements become part of the individual. The movements become part of the individual only when the student can do them without thought and without mistakes. One can then feel the peace and harmony exemplified by becoming the majestic dragon floating above the clouds while performing *Parting the Clouds*. One can feel the confidence, energy, centering, and *chi* that accompanies this movement and others. In addition to these things, one can experience a peaceful strength developed by flowing smoothly and harmoniously, which connects the student with the universal energy within us all. One can experience euphoria through the movements and meditations. These *spiritual* sensations are not forced on anyone, but they are available for those who permit them to happen.

The student can learn to direct his energy as needed. He can learn to use this energy to meditate on personal problems. He can use it to bring relief to aches and pains. He can use this energy to help others. The uses of this energy are endless. The more one becomes involved with the art, the more one realizes the potential for its uses.

One might ask: How can the energy flow be recognized? Once felt, what *good* is it? How can one use it? How can it benefit the individual?

There are several ways to recognize the energy flow. When standing after performing the last movement of the *Stationary Ten*, the student can feel a tremendous rush of energy. It is a tingling sensation throughout the body, up and down the spine, through the back, through the legs, arms, and fingers; there is a lightheadedness. A sense of joy and peace accompanies these movements. Moreover, an increased sense of awareness, a realization that *everything in the universe is unfolding as it should*, and that the individual is part of that unfolding also accompany these physical experiences. But remember, these sensations will not occur unless one is able to do the movements without thought, for they are moving meditations.

Most of the techniques in Gohn Dagow can be moving meditations. Because movement is more restricted in *Parting the Clouds* than in the *Stationary Ten*, the two produce different energy. In *Parting the Clouds* the student does not extend the arms. He bends the legs only slightly. There is no up or down body movement. Thus, the close framework of the individual's own body and energy field contains the energy flow. Because the student holds his arms relatively close to the body, elbows close in, fingers extended and joined, the energy flow is more centering, peaceful and quiet, yet strong, not *tingling*, as in the *Stationary Ten.* The slower the student performs these movements, the more dynamic the energy flow. As with the *Stationary Ten*, the student can feel peace and joy by doing *Parting the Clouds.*

The joy accompanying the flowing energy comes from a center of higher consciousness rather than lower. One feels deep, inner peace and peace with all things, which results from being aware of flowing with the universal life force. The feeling is purely positive. One knows this, and so one follows that feeling.

Once the student experiences the feeling and understands it, the question of "what good is it" is no longer relevant, for the experience itself is enough; (we have already suggested specific uses, i.e., directing energy for healing, etc.).

Also, once the student experiences the feeling, the question of how it can benefit the individual is irrelevant. The benefits will be obvious. The individual can renew his energy to perform daily tasks, or other things that require extra mental or physical energy. His outlook on life will be brighter, and he will project to others that sense of peace and flowing with all things. He will be more at peace with himself and others, and he will be more in control of his words, actions, and emotions, if he so chooses.

Gohn Dagow is not the only path up the mountain, but it is a path that offers the individual a means of total self-development. It is a martial art, but it is much more than martial. Gohn Dagow is an art with philosophical and spiritual dimensions that border on being religious. Because of the philosophical and spiritual basis of the art, the individual can use Gohn Dagow as a life guide, as a means of learning to flow with one's self and others.

The philosophies and the physical techniques are taken from Nature. Nature is the mirror of life through which Man learns about himself. The underlying Gohn Dagow philosophy that *nothing is so permanent as never to change* is constantly reflected in that mirror, and the essence of Gohn Dagow is always to flow with that change and be at peace.

飛 鳥

Bird Flies

Can the bird fly beyond the capacity of its wings?
The bird cannot fly higher than his wings can take him.
However, on occasion, he may soar beyond that point.

Ending/Beginning

With each ending
there is a new beginning.

PHILOSOPHIES INDEX

TECHNIQUES INDEX

USE

E = Energy Flowing
SD = Self Defense
H = Healing
M = Moving Meditation

Ordering Information

Classes and Workshop Inquiry

If you would like additional copies of *Gohn Dagow - Movements for Health and Self Defense*, and they cannot be found in your bookstore, simply send the following information:

Your name ________________________________

Your address ______________________________

City ______________________

State _____________________ **ZIP** __________

Send $11.45 for each copy. Shipping and handling costs are included in the price. Make checks payable to *Flowing Dragon Productions*. Please type or print your name and address legibly. Send your orders to:

Flowing Dragon Productions
P.O. Box 3238
Ashland, OR 97520

(For extra fast delivery, send $13.95 for each copy ordered.)

If you would like information on classes and/or workshops dealing with Gohn Dagow, use the above address and state which subject you wish additional information:

- ☐ Moving/Meditations
- ☐ Healing
- ☐ Self Defense
- ☐ All of the above